ABCs of Wellness

A Guide for Every Childlike Soul

Theresa Flynn

ISBN: 979-8-218-74332-1

"I say unto you, except you be converted, and become as little children, you shall not enter into the kingdom of heaven."

Matthew 18:3

Other Books By TAVI/Theresa Flynn

I Love You, Be Well: A Story of Doing God's Will Without Going Viral

Great Exchanges: The Guidebook for Post Abortion Healing Retreats

Available on Amazon.com or through tavicoachingandwellness.com

DEDICATION

This book is dedicated to everyone, young and old, happy or healing, restored and renewing, who seeks to move forward on the path to God. Read it to learn, read it to teach. Read it to find the joy of the LORD. *Enjoy the journey to treating yourself and others well.*

ACKNOWLEDGEMENTS

Many thanks to Phyllis Hinson of Shiloh Farm Ministry for letting me share my poem years ago, and for loving my kids when they were young. Thanks to Katrina Smith for using her artistic talent to reach those young campers. Thank you to my husband, Joe, for all his help, my beloved and supportive daughter Emily, and every Sister and Brother in Christ who keep me focused on the bigger picture: reaching others for God.

ENDORSEMENT

As a Recovery Pastor, I believe *The ABCs of Wellness* is a beautiful tool for instilling Godly values in the hearts of children—but that's not all. This book also speaks powerfully to adults who are learning to navigate the waters of emotional, spiritual, and relational wellness. Each page offers a scriptural foundation that helps readers understand their feelings, face life's challenges, and build strong moral character. It gently points both young hearts and seasoned souls toward a life anchored in Jesus. It's more than an alphabet—it's a spiritual roadmap for anyone seeking to grow in God's truth and grace.

Pastor Rich Cederman
Bethel Church, Goldsboro NC

Dear Reader:

Thank you for entering the *ABCs of Wellness* world. The vocabulary in this book is, I believe, fundamental to experiencing emotional and spiritual wellness. The poem poured out of me one weekend as I contemplated how simple...yet how profound...it is to live from the childlike heart that Jesus said is so dear to Him in Matthew 18:3.

I share these common emotional and spiritual development concepts with a wide audience: may the LORD's wisdom sing over you! Whether it's a grandparent reading to grandchildren; homeschoolers incorporating the guide into a character-building curriculum; licensed and certified people-helpers working with groups or individuals; or anyone in or out of recovery who has made Christian growth, healing, and change a part of their lifestyle...

Have fun moving through this soul-enriching rhyme. Feel free to read it twice: once for the simple rhyme and once for the Scriptures and commentary. Be well!

Theresa Flynn

Consider This:

Is Jesus your LORD and Savior (John 3:16)?

Is God "large and in charge" in your life right now?

What is your next step in trusting God to be the power source for your life?

It's never too early or too late! God loves you, and if we confess our sins, He is faithful and just to forgive (1 John 1:19).

There is so much more to life with God. May you seek and find it!

A is for ACTION

Make a choice that is good

All day long, you have decisions to make. *Will I do the right thing, or will I ignore my responsibilities? Will I choose to be in a good mood, or will I be negative and lash out at others? Will I ask for help? Will I give it?* The choice really is yours. We all have bad days and bad moods, but taking a simple action can often turn things around. It starts in your heart and mind.

1 Corinthians 10:31

B is for BOUNDARIES

Only do what you should

You are only responsible for your own actions, feelings, and reactions. You are not required to take on others' responsibilities, and you are never the one who causes their feelings and decisions. Really! This is hard for many to accept, and often it's the source of a lot of struggles in our lives. God has given you a job in your family, church, and community, but He also has given everyone else their own as well. We can be of service to others without neglecting ourselves!

Galatians 6:5

C is for COMPASSION

Think of others too

There is no better way out of a bad mood than to think about what someone else is going through. Once you put yourself in their shoes, you can often change your focus and do something nice for somebody else. There is a big reward in our hearts for doing something small for another, especially when we want nothing in return.

Philippians 2:3-4

D is for DIRECTION

Your journey is up to you!

Which way are you pointing? You can turn around any time you think you are headed in the wrong direction. You also can make choices and choose feelings that point you in the right direction, even if those around you are clearly headed for danger.

Proverbs 3:5-6

E is for EXPECTATIONS

Am I asking it right?

You cannot expect things from people that they are unable to give. A baby can't do the laundry, and your boss shouldn't do your work. The more people expect things that simply cannot happen, the more frustrated they can get. If it is your job, do it. If it is someone else's job, they should do it. This big word and big idea goes with "Boundaries" (Letter B).

2 Corinthians 9:8

F is for FEELINGS

They don't have to keep you up at night

Feelings are not always facts! God made you to have feelings, just like He does, but sometimes feelings can take over your life. When you don't know what to do with your feelings, you can talk to someone you trust, you can take them to God (especially when no one is around), and you can wait to see if your feelings change before acting on them. Often they do!

Philippians 4:6-7

G is for GRATITUDE

A big thank you to all

Gratitude means being thankful. Nothing turns around a negative feeling like making the choice to be thankful for *something*. I bet you there is something that you can be thankful for today. In fact, why don't you make a list right now!

Psalm 100:4-5

H is for HELP

Because sometimes we all fall

Asking for help may seem hard, especially if there were times when nobody was there to help you when you needed it. Reaching out and helping somebody else is a great way to be the person you might have needed in the past, and it also makes a friend. Next time you do need help, someone might be happy to help you back.

Luke 10: 25-37

I is for

INTEGRITY

What you do when no one sees

It helps you more than you know to do the right thing, no matter what. Trusting ourselves is important because sometimes we are the only ones we have. When others also trust you, you can be sure that they will be happy to help you make a good life for yourself and the ones you love.

Proverbs 21:3

J is for

JOY

Enjoy the world, the sky, the trees

Joni Eareckson Tada wrote that "joy is peace dancing." Joni has been paralyzed from the shoulders down for most of her life and lives in a wheelchair. If she can think of dancing when she thinks of feeling joy and it doesn't make her sad, then you can choose joy too. Put down the screens and enjoy the beautiful world around you.

Romans 15:13

K is for KINDNESS

A little goes long …

Kindness counts. Sometimes you have to be kind to yourself, too! Eat good food, think good thoughts, and do some stuff. Sometimes you will have an opportunity to be kind to others. In your family, with friends, or even a stranger when it is safe and God is directing. A smile is sometimes all the kindness needed.

Ephesians 4:32

L is for LOVE

God's favorite song

The Bible is all about LOVE! How God made us, loved us enough to give us freedom to live how we want, and even helped us out of the darkness we created by sending His Son Jesus to bring us back to Himself. Jesus said that the two most important commandments are to *love God* with all our hearts, souls, and minds, and to *love our neighbors* as ourselves. This is the kind of love that lasts.

1 John 4:16

M is for MONEY

Be wise and beware

You can earn money, you can save money, and you can spend money. It is important to take this seriously so that you can make plans for your money and meet important goals. Do you know that you make other people money by simply clicking on their posts or apps? Be wise about what and who you let influence you. If you are not comfortable with them getting rich by wasting your own time and damaging your mind...turn it off and turn around.

Proverbs 21:20

N just means NO

It doesn't mean you don't care

If somebody asks you to do something that you fear is not right or that makes you uncomfortable, it is okay to say "No" and to mean it. Checking with the Word of God and with people you trust can help you figure out the best thing to do. Anyone in your life or online who tries to move quickly, or who makes you feel guilty for *not* doing something wrong in God's eyes, is not a safe person. Do what you can to get away from them.

1 Corinthians 10:13

O is for OPINIONS

We all have one, they say

People, including children, are entitled to their opinions and preferences about a lot of things. Learn how to decide if what you are thinking is an opinion or preference, a reaction based on a feeling, or an actual fact. Keeping your opinions to yourself is often the best way to avoid a fight, but we are allowed to have them!

Galatians 1:10

P stands for PRAY

Have you talked to God today?

You may not be able to "see" God, but most of us know that there is something more to our world and our life. This is called meaning and purpose. We all have a Creator who loves us, and He is available 24/7 to talk to. Bring Him your fears, joys, and concerns, and He promises He will never leave or forsake you.

Psalm 145:18

Q is for QUIET

Think a thought the whole way through

Sometimes our days and nights can be very noisy. Work and school, gaming, social media, and TV can follow us everywhere, even in the car and on our pillows at night. It is important to unplug so that your mind can relax and you can hear yourself think and even have the energy to read a book or dream a dream.

Psalm 23

R is for REST

It's important, and that's true

This word goes with "quiet," naturally. Our lives and homes might be very busy and stressed, and we might be, too, but if you unplug and get quiet, you might find that your rest is better and that you have more energy to do the important things and the fun things.

Matthew 11:28-30

S is for SAFETY

If it's wrong, you must tell

Parents, teachers, and leaders should have the safety of children in mind. Adults should be protective of the growing. Those in authority over us should have our interests in mind. Most do their best to keep our world safe. But if there are people you are not safe with, get help to get away. Also, if there are places you take yourself, especially online, that you know are not safe, get away and stay away. It's not worth it!

Psalm 46:1

T is for TIME

Try to spend it well

Don't feel bad if you have wasted time. We all have. Remind yourself that you can start over and spend time wisely with your family, with your work, with your activities and friends, and with God also. Even though time never stops, He gives us a re-do anytime we ask for one. Just ask!

John 9:4-5

U ... means UNBELIEVERS

You can show them the way

We all have to make a choice to believe in God and the goodness of life. Everyone. If you live a purposeful, peaceful life and tell people it's because you know God and want to please Him and share His love with those around you, you just might help unbelievers change their heart and their life. Forever.

Mark 16:15

V is for
VICTORY in Jesus

But under God's wings you must stay

The Bible tells us about a battle, but it's not against people. It's a spiritual battle. As a believer in Jesus, you can put on the Armor of God (Ephesians 6) and ask the LORD for protection, and for the power to love your enemies and forgive those who hurt you. This will protect you and will often help those around you.

1 Corinthians 15:57

W is for Wisdom

It's more precious than gold

As we get to the end of our ABCs, this word sums up the whole book. It is possible to *know* a lot of stuff, to *learn* a lot of stuff, and to *talk about* a lot of stuff, but if you do not have God to provide inner wisdom and the power to live with integrity and gratitude, you still may struggle to get through life well. Seek and follow wisdom!

James 3:13

X ... STAY AWAY

Have the courage to be bold!

There are things that hurt you that you need to stay away from. Bad attitudes and gossip. Influencers that lead you into darkness and not into light and love. People who are making temporary choices that have dangerous, permanent consequences. Ask God for the courage to boldly stay away and say "No!" You are worth a lot to a lot of people, and mostly to God.

Ephesians 5:11

Y is for
YES

Send me LORD, I will go!

Saying yes includes doing those right things and, of course, making a commitment to follow Jesus, the power source for change. He has a plan and a purpose just for you, and your past should not keep you from it. In fact, God will take the good and bad in your life and use it to change you and to help others. You will be a better you, and they will, too!

Isaiah 6:8

Z IS

THE END

Guard your heart, and it will grow

The Lord your God in your midst,
The Mighty One, will save;
He will rejoice over you with gladness,
He will quiet you with His love,
He will rejoice over you with singing.

Zephaniah 3:17

Take the Next Step

Use these pages to create greater self-awareness and to develop your successful strategies to live well with yourself, your God, and with others.

Consider inviting someone trustworthy into the assignment. Look for someone who can provide accountability and wisdom.

A is for Action

What are some things you need to stop doing? What are some actions you need to start taking? What is your level of willingness to commit to it (1 to 10)?

B is for Boundaries

How can you develop stronger boundaries to protect yourself from doing things that are not for you? Good boundaries protect our peace of mind and protect us from the resentments that weak boundaries can cause.

C is for Compassion

What can you do right now for someone else? No matter how big or how small, that one act of service, given out of your abundance, can make the difference in your day and theirs. Don't forget the power of prayer.

D is for Direction

What do you need to tell yourself about the direction your life is heading? Who can help you make sure you are heading in the right direction?

E is for Expectations

How much peace are you losing because you are expecting something that cannot be delivered? Or are you trying to meet the demands of someone's unrealistic expectations? How can you stop?

____

____

____

____

____

____

____

____

____

____

____

____

____

____

____

____

____

____

____

____

____

____

F is for Feelings

Is it a feeling or a fact? How can you tell? Hang in there until you hear the truth from God about it.

G is for Gratitude

List the relationships you are grateful for. Add the ways that God has provided for you and the situations that have turned out well. Thank God for it all!

H is for Help

Ask yourself how good you are at doing what needs to be done. Do you ask for help when you need it? Is there room for improvement, and are you able to help others as well?

I is for Integrity

Where can you practice being your authentic self? What will it look like to do the right thing even if nobody is looking? How can God help? What is your integrity level (1 to 100%)

J is for Joy

Make an appointment with joy. What can you do to make sure you feel God's goodness as you do something positive for yourself and others?

K is for Kindness

What is your plan to be kind to yourself and kind to someone else today? This week? From now on?

L is for Love

Ask God to show you how much He loves you. What does He say about it?

M is for Money

What is your plan for being a good steward of your resources and finances?

N is for NO!

When have you had to say no, and how did it feel? Do you need to practice "healthy NO" more often?

O is for Opinions

How important is it for your opinions to be agreed with? Can you allow others to have theirs?

P is for Prayer

What is your prayer to God for this season of your life?

Q is for Quiet

Tell God and yourself your plan for putting limits on the noise around you.

R is for Rest

How does it feel when you have a moment of genuine rest? Don't forget about being productive, but what would it look like to make godly rest a regular part of your day and week?

S is for Safety

What do you have to let go of…and who do you have to let go of…in order to have safety in your life and relationships?

T is for Time

Develop a plan to spend your time more wisely.

U is for Unbelievers

You were once one. There are many out there. How are you representing God's Kingdom to the lost? What can you do to reach them in truth and love?

V is for Victory

What does your next level of victory look like? Imagine your next success and how you will get there with God's Grace.

W is for Wisdom

Look up some Scriptures about wisdom, Old and New Testament. How can you strengthen your relationship with God so that your Godly wisdom grows?

X … Stay Away!

How can you strengthen your ability to stay away from people, places, things, etc. that are not good for you?

Y means Yes!

When have you said yes to God? How did it feel?
What is He asking you to do now?

Z: Guard your heart and it will grow

What have you learned about God, yourself, and others in your ABCs of Wellness journey?

Scriptures:

Scriptures taken from the New King James Version, Thomas Nelson. Copyright 1982.

A/Action

1 Corinthians 10:31 - Therefore, whether you eat or drink, or whatever you do, do all to the glory of God.

B/Boundaries

Galatians 6:5 - For each one shall bear his own load.

C/Compassion

Philippians 2:3-4 – Let nothing be done through selfish ambition or conceit, but in lowliness of mind let each esteem others better than himself. Let each of you look out not only for his own interests, but also the interests of others.

D/Direction

Proverbs 3:5-6 – Trust in the LORD with all your heart, and lean not on your own understanding; In all your ways acknowledge Him, and He shall direct your paths.

E/Expectations

2 Corinthians 9:8 – And God is able to make all grace abound toward you, that you, always having all sufficiency in all things, may have an abundance for every good work.

F/Feelings

Philippians 4:6-7 – Be anxious for nothing, but in everything by prayer and supplication, with thanksgiving, let your requests be made known to God; and the peace of God, which surpasses all understanding, will guard your hearts and minds through Christ Jesus.

G/Gratitude

Psalm 100:4-5 – Enter into His gates with thanksgiving, and into His courts with praise. Be thankful to Him, and bless his name. For the LORD is good; His mercy is everlasting, and His truth endures to all generations.

H/Help

Luke 10:36-37 – This is the story of the Good Samaritan. "So which of these three do you think was neighbor to him who fell among the thieves? And he said, "He who showed mercy on him." Then Jesus said to him, "Go and do likewise."

I/Integrity

Proverbs 21:3 – To do righteousness and justice is more acceptable to the LORD than sacrifice.

J/Joy

Romans 15:13 – Now may the God of hope fill you with all joy and peace in believing, that you may abound in hope by the power of the Holy Spirit.

K/Kindness
Ephesians 4:32 – And be kind to one another, tenderhearted, forgiving one another, even as God in Christ forgave you.

L/Love
1 John 4:16 – And we have known and believed the love that God has for us. God is love, and he who abides in love abides in God, and God in him.

M/Money
Proverbs 21:20 – There is desirable treasure, and oil in the dwelling of the wise, but a foolish man squanders it.

N/NO
1 Corinthians 10:13 No temptation has overtaken you except what is common to mankind. And God is faithful; he will not let you be tempted beyond what you can bear. But when you are tempted, he will also provide a way out so that you can endure it.

O/Opinions
Galatians 1:10 – For do I now persuade men, or God? Or do I seek to please men? For if I still pleased men, I would not be a bondservant of Christ.

P/Pray

Psalm 145:18 – The LORD is near to all who call upon Him, to all who call upon Him in truth.

Q/Quiet

Psalm 23 – The LORD is my shepherd; I shall not want. He makes me to lie down in green pastures; He leads me beside the still waters. He restores my soul; He leads me in paths of righteousness for His name's sake. Yea, though I walk through the valley of the shadow of death, I will fear no evil; for You are with me; Your rod and Your staff, they comfort me. You prepare a table before me in the presence of my enemies; You anoint my head with oil; My cup runs over. Surely goodness and mercy shall follow me all the days of my life; And I will dwell in the house of the LORD forever.

R/Rest

Matthew 11:28-30 – Come to Me, all you who labor and are heavy laden, and I will give you rest. Take My yoke upon you and learn from Me, for I am gentle and lowly in heart, and you will find rest for your souls. For My yoke is easy and My burden is light.

S/Safety

Psalm 46:1 – God is our refuge and strength, a very present help in trouble.

T/Time

John 9:4-5 – I must work the works of Him who sent Me while it is day; the night is coming when no one can work. As long as I am in the world, I am the light of the world.

U/Unbelievers

Mark 16:15 – And He said to them, "Go into all the world and preach the gospel to every creature."

V/Victory

1 Corinthians 15:57 – But thanks be to God, who gives us the victory through our Lord Jesus Christ.

Ephesians 6 describes the "whole armor of God" as the belt of truth, the breastplate of righteousness, the preparation of the gospel of peace on our feet, the shield of faith, the helmet of salvation, and the sword of the Spirit, which is the word of God.

W/Wisdom

James 3:13 – Who is wise and understanding among you? Let them show it by their good life, by deeds done in the humility that comes from wisdom.

X/STAY AWAY

Ephesians 5:11 – And have no fellowship with the unfruitful works of darkness, but rather expose them.

Y/Yes

Isaiah 6:8 – Also I heard the voice of the LORD saying, "Whom shall I send? And who will go for us?" Then I said, "Here am I. Send me!"

Z/The End

Zephaniah 3:17 – The LORD your God in your midst, the Mighty One, will save; He will rejoice over you with gladness, He will quiet you with His love, He will rejoice over you with singing.

NOTES:

____

____

____

____

____

____

____

____

____

____

____

____

____

____

____

NOTES:

NOTES:

NOTES:

NOTES:

NOTES:

NOTES:

About the Author

Theresa Flynn MABC CPLC has been living a lifestyle of salvation, recovery, and healing for 20 years as of 2025. She is the owner of TAVI Coaching and Wellness LLC, which serves online and in-person individuals, couples, and groups with certified Christian Life Coaching, Biblical Counsel & Care, and consulting. Experiencing a renewed mind and victorious living is the surprise blessing of her life, and her desire is to lead others to God so they can experience this as well. She attends church regularly and volunteers in several healing ministries. She lives in Eastern North Carolina with her husband, daughter, and fur babies.

www.ingramcontent.com/pod-product-compliance
Lightning Source LLC
LaVergne TN
LVHW061253100826
845148LV00008B/1115
* 9 7 9 8 2 1 8 7 4 3 3 2 1 *